GROWING UP

IN JERSEY CITY

By

COSMO F. FERRARA

First published in United States by SwagKirby LLC

Printed in New York, NY 2025

ISBN: 979-8-9923333-1-2

Dedication

This collection of memories is dedicated first to Mom and Dad, who

worked so hard to give me love, discipline, education, and a sense of

values; to my brothers, Jack and Joe (hereafter referred to as "Sims"),

who were always there to talk with or play ball with; to my relatives

and friends who gave me a feeling of belonging; to the neighbors,

teachers, priests, shopkeepers, and the many nameless but recognizable

people who added color and continuity to my life; to all who made

Jersey City so much more than a place, and who made growing up

there so much fun. And to my wife Fran, who has shared so many

pleasant hours with me recalling our youth Downtown.

TABLE OF CONTENTS

OUR HOUSE

My neighborhood in downtown Jersey City would probably be
called a ghetto. Except for a few Polish and Irish families, most of the
people on my block were of Italian extraction, and all the families were
catholic. I knew very few Protestants or Jews as a kid. I suppose this
kind of isolation limits one's view of the world, but it also makes
growing up a lot easier.

Most of the people lived in three-and four-story buildings filled
with relatives. So a kid growing up in this neighborhood would have
plenty of aunts and uncles and cousins living right in the same building.
In our house, for example, my grandmother and Aunt Mary lived on the
second floor, we lived on the third, and my Aunt Lena, Uncle Frank,
and two cousins, Andrew and Jack, lived on the fourth. This
arrangement stayed the same for the first twenty years of my life. We
were five boys living on the third and fourth floors in that house, and
Grandma knew the footsteps of each of us. On Sunday morning she
would often let us know who came home the latest the night before.
"You're the youngest," I remember her saying to me a few times, "how
come you're last to come home?"

The first floor was the only one in our house that changed hands.
And for most of the years it was occupied by young cousins who had

just gotten married. My Aunt Lillie and Uncle Nick lived in their own house down the street with their children, most of whom were older than I. As these cousins got married, it seemed their first love nest was the first floor in "Grandma's house." They'd stay for a short while until they could get together enough money for a larger apartment or a home of their own, or until they had too many babies for the small apartment.

People made friends easily with others on the block. My parents, for example, had some friends just a few doors away for most of their lives. The men had a Friday night poker game that travelled from one home to another for more years than I can remember. They would play from about seven-thirty to eleven, at which time the wives would join them for coffee and a sandwich. Mom also had a club of her own, women she had known since her teenage years. They didn't play cards but just talked. My brother Jack dubbed them the "Blah Blah Club" because they talked non-stop. Nice people, though, really nice people. I'm sure these gatherings got to be somewhat boring sometimes, but more often I'm sure they were a night out with people you could be comfortable with, who shared the same problems, fears, ambitions you had.

One of my fondest memories is of Sunday mornings, when my parents' friends would stop at our house for coffee or a drink. These mornings were for men only, though, as the women were at home getting dinner ready. My father was always glad to see them, and so was my mother, most of the time. The bottle would go on the table and the coffeepot would go on the stove. There'd be a twist on the cheek for me by these hard-working men with the strong rough hands. I wouldn't mind, though, because by Tuesday or Wednesday the red pock mark on my face would be gone. The men would kibitz and chatter, about what I don't recall, because I didn't really pay attention to the particulars. But their being there gave everybody a good feeling, a special feeling that added to Sunday's being a special day.

Having relatives and friends close by gave people the support systems they needed to get through the hard times. My mother tells the story of the night my appendix almost burst. It was over Christmas vacation and what began as nausea in the morning had developed into agonizing pain by evening. By the time the doctor came to the house (remember those days!) it was about nine o'clock at night. Doctor Skrypsky said I should go to the hospital right away for an appendectomy. My mother said she wanted to call my Aunt Lena from upstairs. The doctor, who knew the family very well after treating us all for so many years, said in his gruff but understanding manner, "I don't care who you call but this boy has to go to the hospital now." Mom didn't skip a beat and said, "I just want her to stay with the other kids." That wasn't really the case and the doctor probably knew it. Mom wanted the advice of another woman, a mother. She wanted the words of encouragement one needs at a crucial time, and she got them from Aunt Lena who was just upstairs.

I have many memories of people sitting around the kitchen table, coffee cups in hand, discussing someone's illness, a financial crisis, a problem teen-ager. More often though the gatherings were pleasant experiences. I remember that for years I spent New Year's Eve downstairs at Grandma's with my parents and brothers and a good many of my aunts, uncles, and cousins. Every year I'd wait for Aunt Flossie to say, "Next year we're all going to see Guy Lombardo." At midnight we'd open the windows and bang pots and pans to cheer the New Year in. There'd be toasts, and hugs and kisses, and fried sausage on Italian bread. I can still taste it! My cousins who were older would call in to say Happy New Year to their parents, and some would even leave the party they were at to come over to Grandma's and pay their respects in person. Same might call our existence "provincial" and confining, but it was also secure, warm, am loving. Not a bad atmosphere to grow up in.

STREET SCENES

If you lived in the city when I did, you probably remember fruits and vegetables being sold from trucks that made their way slowly from one block to another. You may even recall vaguely the predecessor of the produce truck, the horse-drawn wagon. "Peddlers" would announce their presence, singing out, "Water-mell-on." They'd advertise the day's specials on large paper bags tacked to wooden posts at the corners of the flat-bed: "PEARS 3 lbs. 39C." Women in housedresses would come to the truck to shop or just call out from a window and have the boy bring up peaches, lettuce, and spinach.

As a kid I was fascinated by the way they collected garbage. Before the mechanized garbage truck was invented, one man stood in a large, open-topped bin and caught the trash barrels tossed up to him by his partner. He'd dump the trash at his feet and toss the empty barrel back. As he made his rounds the pile in the bin would grow, raising the "dumper" higher and higher off the ground.

Common around election time were the red, white and blue cars with "Vote Row B" painted on them. They'd roll endlessly through the streets, and from their loudspeakers a monotone voice would exhort people to vote to preserve the good life or to vote for this year's

Reform candidate. There was always a reform candidate in Jersey City- and probably with good reason. Then, too, there were the street corner rallies, complete with bandstands but without bands. Rallies would be held in the evening around these stands but the crowds were always rather sparse, and those who were there showed little indication of believing anything that was said, except for maybe a few young kids. And then only rarely.

A familiar scene on our street was a neighbor walking to the Tammany Tavern in slippers, to have his white enamel pot filled with fresh brew which he brought home to be had with supper. You'd hear the twelve o'clock whistle and see the girls from Pennick's walking home for lunch in their blue cotton uniforms. There'd be guys pitching pennies and girls playing hopscotch or jumping rope or rocking baby carriages. Mothers would call their children from third story windows and drop money down to them in balls of paper, on which were written the items to be fetched from the store.

Religious processions were a regular summer event in our neighborhood. Leading the entourage would be a statue of the saint being honored, held aloft by teams of burly young men. Then would come the patient priest, the altar boys whose expressions made it clear they'd rather be playing baseball, the little girls in white communion dresses, the old women in their black hats, and Professor Olivetti's Marching Band. And of course there'd be someone carrying a banner bearing the image of St. Rocco or St. Anthony or whatever saint was being honored that day. People from the sidewalk would donate dollar bills that would be pinned to the banner in outrageous display.

In the evening there would be "a festa," the feast to continue the religious celebration. Two or three city blocks would be closed off to traffic and filled with booths and stands; with the aroma of fried zeppoli and Italian sausage and peppers; and with the sounds of the "big wheel" spinning, kids squealing in delight, the music of Professor Olivetti's Band, and the chatter of hundreds of people enjoying a happy summer ritual.

Another street scene I recall dimly was from just after the war. A one-armed man walked through the neighborhood singing plaintive songs through a megaphone. People would occasionally toss a few coins to him which he'd deftly catch through the fat end of the megaphone, slide down to the smaller end, and transfer to his hand and then his pocket.

In winter, ashes from coal-and wood-burning stoves would be sprinkled over icy sidewalks and stoops to keep people from slipping. Snow would be piled at curbside in mounds five feet high and stay there, seemingly for weeks. Garbage barrels would stand where the snow had been to preserve a hard-earned parking space. Most drivers seemed to respect those barrels and the work they represented.

Sledding in the street, or what kids called sleigh-riding, was common. Sometimes we'd walk up to Dickinson or to Cemetery Hill, but often we'd just do our sledding in the street. With the Flexible Flyer tightly in hand, we'd run as fast as we could on the icy street, toss the sled down and then throw ourselves on it, belly first, to catch a short ride.

Other familiar sights include another hauling a bicycle or baby carriage up the stoop, kids cooling off under the open fire hydrant until the cops came to shut it. There were people sweeping their sidewalks and the curb in front of them. And remember the aroma of the burning leaves they'd collect in fall? On Saturday we'd see men washing their cars and then driving to the shade of the Pennick's factory to polish them. In spring and fall you'd see housewives perched precariously on window ledges forty or fifty feet off the ground washing their windows. There were always double-parked cars, and men gathering outside the Tammany as early as eleven-thirty on Sunday morning to wait for the one o'clock opening.

Constant on most summer evenings were two trucks. One was

Mr. Softee, playing its insidious chimes, "Hooray for Mr. Softee." The

other was the truck carrying the smallest merry-go-round ever made. It

was no more than six feet in diameter and had four or five tiny horses

on it. From its loudspeaker came always the same song, "Come Ona

My House." But like the Pied Piper it drew little kids, who came with

nickel in hand for a few minutes on the carousel.

There were same people in my neighborhood who never left the

block. They'd sit at windows or maybe venture to the top step of the

front stoop. I guess there was enough life in those street scenes to

entertain them.

SATURDAY MORNING IN SPRING

Saturday morning in spring was a time for baseball. Even when the erratic winds of March and April chilled the bones, and catching a fastball could sting all day, it was spring and time to oil up the old glove and start playing baseball.

For weeks already we had been reading about our Giants in Phoenix, our Yankees in Fort Lauderdale, and our Dodgers in Vero Beach. We could wait no longer.

In the early morning quiet, my brother Jack and I would walk down to Joe Paone's candy Store to meet Marty and Googsie and the other Battler Juniors from our neighborhood. They were all three or four years older than I, so I had to mind my place and speak only at carefully selected moments if I wanted to play. And I sure did want to play.

Though not a regular, I wore the same uniform they did-a blue baseball cap with a red bill. The crown of my cap was dashingly creased to enhance my stature. This crease was achieved by folding the crown over the bill, wrapping the hat around a large water glass, binding the whole thing with a handkerchief, and letting it sit for an eternity (two or three days) until the cap held a pennant shape.

After five or six kids gathered, we'd start to make our way to the field, Oakley Oval, a couple of acres of grassless dirt doused with oil to keep the dust from flying all over the city. I could taste the camaraderie as we'd move toward the field, in the street all the way. The guys would toss a ball back and forth as we walked, predicting victory or giving exaggerated accounts of on-the-field exploits. Someone would dash ahead and call for a "long, high one." My role was chasing errant throws or crawling under parked cars after someone's miss. Most often though I just carried the bats while biding my time.

At the field my excitement would rise with the tension, wondering if I'd get to play. Over and over I'd count heads-"5-6-7. Only seven. If nobody else shows up, I'll play. Better warm up." I became a pretty decent fielder because while the others took batting practice, I was permitted to chase down the long belts in the outfield. I'd dash after the ball, scoop it up, and whip it in as ham as I could. Then I'd look around, only to find that no one was watching.

While the other team was completing its warmups, and our captains were making out the line-up, I'd casually stand near-by, pounding my Eddie Joost fielder's glove or swinging a bat, hoping they'd notice and include me. A few times when I thought I was a shoo-in--or when Jack came over and whispered, "I think you're playing today"-the blood would rush to my head as my stomach dropped.

On some occasions, with excitement charging through my system, a roar would go up at the last minute: "Hey, here comes Tommy. Yeah, Tommy, we need you. We don't have enough guys." And out they would stride, Tommy in my place, and me arranging the bats on the sideline.

But once in a while I'd get a chance to play. Right field, of course, because there were few lefty hitters in our neighborhood. I'd charge out there like Enos Slaughter and limber up, mentally preparing myself to make a diving catch, or to race to my right to cut off a single, wheel, and rifle a strike to the plate to gun down the runner trying-foolishly-to score from second.

In reality, though, right field was pretty uneventful. And batting ninth in the order, I was told to crouch down at the plate and wait for a walk. Already three inches shorter than anyone else on the field, I resented having to get any lower. Often I'd stand in a crouch until the pitcher's release and then straighten up for a swing. I knew I could hit and all I needed was one sharp single through the box to prove it.

But they'd yell, "Crouch, crouch down, he'll walk ya." To stay in the game I crouched, but I seldom walked. Usually I struck out-looking. Strike-outs and no catches-my stats for the day. But stats don't show everything, and in my case they couldn't begin to show anything of the joy and excitement I derived from the game. Even with the strike-outs, I was as happy as the kid who hit a grand slammer. Things couldn't possibly be more right. It was Saturday morning, in spring, and I was playing baseball.

THE WEDDING

In all honesty, I don't remember attending any football weddings. While the weddings I went to, even as a young boy, were not very elaborate affairs, they were always more than beer and sandwich parties. Not that the menu was nouvelle cuisine. Mostly it was two thin slabs of roast beef smothered in brown gravy, with mashed potatoes and string beans or peas, a pitcher of wine or beer for the adults and a pitcher of soda-sometimes birch beer, a rare commodity-for us kids. Standard but hearty fare for unpretentious working-class people.

Back then, kids were invited to weddings, I guess because the cost-per-head was not so prohibitive. Most of the receptions I went to were held in a square, plain room behind Coletta's tavern. A blue clothe hung above the small stage, bearing a congratulatory message to the bride and groom, written in white letters covered with silver sparkles. On each side of "Congratulations Marie and Joseph" would be the papier mache wedding bells. A bell also dangled from the revolving crystal globe that hung from the ceiling at the center of the hall.

There wasn't much for kids to do at weddings except drink soda and observe the goings-on. For example, the dancing. I liked when friends of the bridal couple attended the weddings because they were often good dancers and I loved watching a young, exuberant pair do a neat "jitterbug," as my parents called it. I yearned to be ten years older so I could come to a family wedding with a pretty girl and jitterbug like that. Invariably you'd see a young boy like myself pressed into dancing with his mother or maiden aunt, the two proceeding distressingly around the floor, his head held tightly to her bosom. More often than not the women would dance with one another, especially if the band played a polka, an infrequent request at an Italian wedding.

The men would gravitate toward one another, often to the rear of the hall close to the bar. There'd be a lot of good-natured mocking and kibitzing, especially with relatives from Long Island.

"When are you coming to see us?"

"We came to see you last time."

"That was two years ago."

"That's alright, it's still your turn to come see us."

"I came here tonight."

"That don't count. You've gotta come to the house."

"Nobody ever comes to see us."

"Who the hell told you to live way the hell out to the sticks?"

Kids soon tired of the "adult" world, and off would come the clip-on ties and the two-tone jackets newly bought from The Wonder store or S. Klein on the Square. They'd start running and playing tag and you'd hear, "I'm gonna call your father."

A feature at my earliest weddings was the entertainment. I had a few cousins who could sing and seized every opportunity to do so. Sooner or later someone would start the rhythmic chant, "We want Charlie." It might have been Charlie himself who started it, but without too much coaxing Charlie would soon be in serious discussion with the band. He must have been in his early teens then, a handsome kid with wavy reddish hair, and a decent voice. But more than that he had confidence and showmanship. As he grew older Charlie's repertoire included a lot of Sinatra, but in the early years it was just Jolson. When he'd get down on one knee, spread out his hands, and with all the emotion his body could muster belt out, "I'd walk a million miles / for one of your smiles / my Ma-a-mmy," Charlie would bring down the house.

Another feature of the weddings was the "boosta" line. About three-quarters into the evening, the mother of the bride would give her daughter the signal to stop table-hopping and go sit with her husband at the dais. The guests would know this was the time to line up to give the couple their "envelopes" and best wishes. The women would round up their husbands who grudgingly tagged along to perform this chore. "Fix your hair, and straighten that tie."

The boosta line was tacky but efficient. People were honest about the fact that the wedding celebration was the time to help the young couple on its way and this was how to do it. I'm sure as people made their way toward the bridal couple they recalled their own wedding, their hopes, their plans, and the disappointments that followed. And I'm sure they were truly wishing tonight's couple a life filled with greater prosperity and fewer heartaches than their own. But they realized that, on balance, this couple's fortunes would be pretty much the same as their own and they wanted this couple to know support would be there when they needed it.

The couple would respond with a tiny box containing an ash tray or wine glass bearing the inscription: "Theresa and Frank June 3, 1949." The box was often tied with a ribbon, and affixed to it was a little mesh basket containing "wedding candy." I collected as many of these candies as I could because I loved the sweet taste of the sugar coating and the pleasant crunch of biting into it.

"Good Night, Sweetheart" would signal the end of the affair, though it probably wasn't necessary. As you looked around the hall you'd see a few kids asleep on their mothers laps, and one or two men who had a little too much to drink slouched uncomfortably on stiff wooden chairs, sound asleep and snoring loudly. The women would be kissing one another good-bye and the men would still be arguing over who should come visit whom.

Going home there might be talk about how good it was to see the cousins, or about who was too sick to make the wedding, or who was still angry with whom and so stayed away deliberately. But often there was just silence, each of us focusing on our own experience at the wedding.

ROOSEVELT STADIUM

Jersey City's Roosevelt Stadium was a WPA project that worked. It was a beautiful structure, away from the hub-ub of the city, affording sports fans the cool though sometimes odoriferous breezes of Newark Bay. It was also a great place to watch a ballgame. The Stadium gave people the feeling of going same place special when they went there to see a game. And so many people did.

My earliest memory of Roosevelt Stadium is very dim because I was very young. I went with my brother Jack and two uncles, Red and Sonny, to see the Jersey City Giants. (My father had not yet developed an interest in baseball. That only came later with the advent of television, when he was forced to watch baseball because his sons were avid fans. As my Uncle Red tells the story, I kept asking him when someone was going to hit a home run. I wanted so much to see a home run. Finally someone did send one out of the park, but I missed it. I was busy looking for the hot dog man, my uncle says, and never saw the ball fly over the fence.

That version probably is accurate because the vendors were part of the stadium's attraction for a young boy. I admired the hot dog vendors in particular, the way they could put the dog in the bun and slap mustard on it in one deft motion. (In those days hot dogs did not come prepackaged as they do at games today.) I'd follow the dog along the human chain to its destination, a hungry young fan ten or twelve seats in, then follow the money back to the vendor. People would begin to get annoyed if the vendor had to send back change.

My attention was also diverted from the playing field by the flags bordering the roof of the stadium, pennants of the teams that made up the International League-teams like the Buffalo Bisons, Newark Bears, Rochester Red Wings, Montreal Maple leafs.

Though I was young and had seen a lot of sandlot baseball, two things surprised me about games at Roosevelt Stadium. One was that the secorrl game of a double header was only seven innings. The other was that only one game was being played on the field. I was used to seeing two or three games being played on two or three intersecting diamonds. It was perfectly acceptable in my neighborhood for the left fielder of one game to be stationed behind the pitcher of another, keeping one eye on the game he was playing in and the other on the game he was standing in the middle of. What a luxury, I thought, to play one game to a field.

Of the Giants games I remember little. For some reason the name Jack Lohrke has stayed with me and Tookie Somebody. And I do recall seeing Wes Westrum, before he went over to New York. But I'll never forget the excitement of being there, of hearing the crack of the bat and the jeering of the crowd, of breathing in the aroma of hot dogs and mustard and professional baseball.

My most vivid memories of Roosevelt stadium involve football. I started going to high school football games when I was in about sixth or seventh grade and vaguely recall getting free passes for the first St. Peter's game each year from somebody or other. There were Ferris games on Friday nights and Prep games on Sunday, even before I was in high school. Once I entered St. Peter's, Sunday ritual included church in the morning and Prep football in the afternoon. On Thanksgiving Day, turkey was a mere incidental. The Prep-Dickinson game at the stadium was the main course.

But the most thrilling of all were the St. Peter's-Memorial clashes. Long before I was a Petrean I remember the likes of Jackie Hyatt and Bobby Schwarz battling the Simunovich brothers and the rest of Joe Coviello's nationally-ranked powerhouse from West New York. Forever implanted firmly but painfully in my memory is the day Mike Mollo snatched victory from the Prep's hands with a long TD run with only seconds on the clock. Memorial rooters danced jubilantly while the Prep faithful stood frozen in shock. People today would be incredulous at the thought of crowds of 20,000 to 25,000 at a high school game in New Jersey. But in those days of my youth that's what that game would draw. Obviously they were not all students or alumni. Anybody in Hudson County who liked sports was at that game.

Yes, Roosevelt Stadium provided the setting for great games and great memories for thousands of people. I'm glad to be one of them.

NICKNAMES

One of the real points of charm in life Downtown was the nicknames people had. For many I never knew their real names. They had always been just Hop, Dinky, Googsie, Chippie, Jed, or Sonny Boy. Nicknames were so common, you never gave a second thought to a Christian name. There were names like Bazooka, Lemons, and Taffy. In one family you had Gumbo, Dekay, Bingalow, and something that sounded like Footers. And how about Eight Ball and his brother Itchie? And names like Eggie, Pinkey, and Sheets?

Often it was body features and size that led to a nickname. Of course there was an assortment of Fats (with variations such as Horse, Chubby, Pudgy, and Jumbo). There were Leftys, Whiteys, Shortys and Skinnys. Mus was short for Muscles, a skinny kid who in same circles was known as swords. There were Dimples, Legs, and Pepper (a red-headed kid). House was a mountain of a man. His son? Half a House. Ox got his name from either his size or his mental capacity. Patty Lamps was so named because of his big eyes, Ming because of his round Oriental-shaped face and narrow eyes, and Sabu from his very dark skin. Ten-after-Ten had feet that rested at 45 degree angles like the hands of a clock at ten-after-ten. Another fellow with the same footwork was Jimmy Ducks.

Larry Squints could barely see an::l Timber was tall and thin. Wiggles was a fat kid whose big behind did just that when he walked. Joey Gogs wore thick eyeglasses that looked like goggles, and Patty Brush always wore a crew-cut. But the most outstanding feature of all was the nose. Big beaks were the inspiration for names like Willie Bruiser and Joe Bugles.

Still others got their names from habits or mannerisms. Like the nervous guy they called Georgie Ulcers, and Nicky Perks, the coffee fiend, and Danny Duals, the hot-rodder. A happy-go-lucky kid with a constant smile was dubbed Cheese. At the other extreme were Hard Times and Nicky Blues, the eternal pessimists. Parsley was into everything, and Sox could give you the batting average of everyone who ever played for the Boston Red Sox. Trigger liked to play cowboys long after he should have. And a name that needs no explanation, Frankie Fots.

Mambo was the son of a band leader and Sally Pups the son of a hot dog vendor. There were Cha Cha Lil and Fingers and Broadway Jimmy. And the Senator, Joe Baa, and Tony Glue, whose name was Pace, often mispronounced as Paste. Who was christened John Ricci (pronounced Richie). He was never referred to as John but as Ricci

(Richie). If you asked, "Did you see Ricci?" the reply would often be,

"Richie Who?" so to make things easier he became "Who".

A lot of nicknames were variations of real names, such as

Pheenie, Flossie, Beattie, and Rocky. Same were modifications of

Italian sir names, like Cher-eek (Cherico), Yappy (Yapiola), TaTa

(Tartaglia}, Graz (Grazioso} and Bal (Balestieri). Some were direct

translations such as Shoes (Scarpa) and The Hand (LaManna). And

don't forget Johnny Bianca Lina, the bleach man.

When you get into reminiscing, names and sometimes faces start

coming back. Names like Weasel, Beans, Zup, Ike, and Colors, the wild

dresser; Spuds, Flint, Sally Moe, Fifi, Fritz, Soupie, Winch, Six, and

Archie. And what about Cloud, Moozie, Billy Bones, Mickey Wheels,

Tiger, and Freddie the Frog? Of course there were Bange, Gunps,

Snookie, Sims, and Dee Dee (later Deed). And sure, Coppo, too.

Some of these names belonged to people I knew personally,

some to people who added to the colorful background of my youth.

Great names reflecting the color and imagination of a people, time and

place I will never forget.

THE KITCHEN

Growing up, I remember the kitchen as the center of activity in our house. That might have been because for a time the only source of heat in our apartment was the big black cast iron stove in the kitchen. It burned coal which my father and brother would bring up from the cellar every night. Once it burned shredded wheat, which I begged for so I could get a decoder ring or something that I heard advertised on the radio. The prize was a big disappointment, as I recall, and I hated the shredded wheat, so Mom used it for fuel.

The stove was set on a base of white tiles, the kind that are now fashionable in Yuppie bars, am that little kids liked to run their toy trucks on. To the left of the stove stood a tall water heater, which Dad always kept painting a shiny silver. One of my few heroic moments in life came when I was about eight years old, and my brother Joe was crawling around the floor am discovered the valve on the heater. He turned it and water began gushing out. I quickly rushed over and shut the valve, preventing what everyone said would have been a major catastrophe.

To the right of the stove was my father's rocker, where he sat in the cozy warmth to read his paper. In summer, however, the rocker was moved over to the window, from which Dad could look out over the roofs of the small houses directly behind ours and across the yards to the rear of the taller buildings on Eighth Street. It was on that rocker in the kitchen that my father taught Jack to sing "God Bless America" and that he tricked all of us with his "watch the smoke come out of my ears" routine. Where he also told me the story of Cinderella in such a distinctive style that, legend has it, I objected to Aunt Cammie's version when she skipped the flourish of trumpets. Dad always provided all the sound effects, including the "bap-a-pata-bap-a-ta-pa."

It was in the kitchen that we ate all of our meals, naturally, and that my parents shared coffee or a drink with friends who'd drop in after church on Sunday morning. From my bedroom just off the kitchen I overheard same serious conversations my parents had there with relatives, over matters such as a cousin's planned marriage outside the faith, an uncle's elopement, arrangements for Grandma's funeral. But there were more good times than sad in that kitchen. We celebrated Thanksgiving there every year with so many relatives Dad had to improvise another table by laying a sheet of plywood (normally used for the trains at Christmas) across two wooden horses. We were crowded but never uncomfortable.

The kitchen was the setting for my father's Friday night poker games with his friends of many years, their wives coming by at the end of the night for coffee-and. We celebrated birthdays in that kitchen and graduations and events of all kinds. Perhaps even more special to me was Sunday dinner, an afternoon ritual that began at eleven o'clock by dipping Italian bread in the gravy and stealing a meatball.

My brother Sims and I shared a quiet lunch there on schooldays. When he was in kindergarten, and I in eighth grade, Mom went out to work. I'd pick Sims up at lunchtime, we'd stop at Annie's to get the paper Dad had left for ire in the morning, and home we'd go. Our sandwiches would be in the refrigerator, our glasses for milk on table. Mom would leave a nickel on Joe's glass and a dime on mine for a treat on the way back to school. We'd have a very civilized lunch, as I'd read The News and Sims a comic book. We'd put the glasses in the sink, say goodbye to Grandma, and go back to school.

It was in the kitchen that I did my homework for so many years. After supper, after my brothers or I took a turn at wiping the dishes, the three of us would lay the books out on the kitchen table and get to work. Dad would be in his rocker reading the paper and Mom would be ironing clothes or doing her beading. In those days Mom worked at home beading sweaters. She'd affix a patterned clothe to four lengths of wood and rest these on two wooden horses. A long thread stacked with sequins or beads of various types was attached to a small wooden-handled needle. Using the needle she'd tediously punch holes in the cloth, sewing the beads to it. I can still hear the steady "pock pock pock" of that needle puncturing the cloth.

In the background we'd hear same of the great radio shows-"The Lone Ranger," "Boston Blackie," "The Shadow," and my favorite, "The Fat Man." "He steps on the scale: weight, 290 pounds; fortune: danger." The radio was almost a constant in that kitchen. In the mornings it was Clavan and Finch, Don Mc Neil's Breakfast Club, Arthur Godfrey, and Martin Block's "Make Believe Ballroom." On Sundays, oddly enough, we listened to Hank Williams, Webb Pierce, Patsy Kline and other country favorites.

The kitchen was the all-purpose room. In winter, when it was too cold to hang clothes outside to dry, they'd hang from a line stretched across the kitchen. Dr. Skrypsky examined sore throats on the kitchen table and that's where business was conducted with the insurance man, the milk man, and Mr. Braun, the jeweler. My brother Jack and I played our first basketball game there, propping a baseball cap above the kitchen door and tossing a crumpled ball of paper into it. It was there that Mom and Dad set down plans to buy the business and that they read, over and over to all who entered there, Jack's letters when he was away at college and on cruises. Small and humble as it was, that kitchen brimmed with the life and am love and warmth that fond memories are made of.

AT THE MOVIES

The first movie theater I remember going to was The Palace on Newark Avenue in Jersey City. Admission was sixteen cents.

The Palace was only a few blocks from my grandmother's house on Fifth Street. Often on a Saturday or Sunday, while my mother and father visited, my brother Jack and I would walk over to the movies. In those days we never checked the movie timetable in the papers. Whenever it was convenient, off we'd go. Entering at the beginning, the middle, or the end of the movie didn't matter. Whatever we missed, we'd pick up the next time around and piece it all together. That was the reason for continuous performances, wasn't it?

The Palace always had a double feature, Pathe News, a cartoon or two, a serial, and coming attractions. During the coming attractions you'd invariably hear, "I'm comin'," as young movie fans were enticed into next week's features. The serials, of course, ran from week to week and here again it didn't really matter to us if we had seen the previous episodes. It was always pretty easy to spot the good guys from the bad guys-the white hat was a tip-off-and we could quickly pick up the threads of the plot.

All of the serials and most of the features at The Palace were adventures, like cowboy movies with Johnny Mack Brown, Red Ryder, or Lash l.aRue. Or swashbucklers, adventures on the high seas, with the likes of the dour Victor Mature or the ever-smiling Errol Flynn. In most of those Pirate movies there was always a beautiful woman on board, often the lovely Patricia Medina in a low-cut gown of the period. She was there against her will, of course, and against the wishes of Captain Blood, or whoever Errol happened to be that week. He'd tolerate the situation, even give out with his haughty "Ha Ha," but she resisted and complained at every tum. Until, of course, they both fell in love.

The confrontation scenes were the best. The two ships would sidle up to one another, firing cannon blasts back and forth. Then Errol's men would climb the ropes and swing out over the turbulent sea onto the decks of the other ship for dueling and hand-to-hand combat. I loved it!

Kids were known to spend an entire day at The Palace, affectionately referred to as "'The Itchhouse." ("Go in with an itch, come out with a scratch.") Late in the afternoon, ushers would move throughout the theater row by row, shining their flashlights on ticket stubs. From the stubs they could tell how long you'd been there, and send you out if you overstayed your welcome.

One of the added features of The Palace was a leaflet advertising coming attractions. Complete with pictures and advertising hype, this little 6x9 leaflet made you walk home filled with anticipation for next week's thrills.

As I got older I branched out and started going to the Capitol with my friends. It was a longer walk down Newark Avenue, but this gave us more time for jostling one another as we made our way to the theater, sometimes eight or ten strong. War movies seemed to be the rage then, just after World War II. After seeing The Steel Helmet, the cry all the way home was "there's a million of 'em."

As we hit the teenage years, we approached the big time-the wide expanse of Journal Square. Though Christopher Columbus was directing us to the Loew's (pronounced Low-ees), there were choices. And besides the choices in movies at The Square, there was splendor in the theaters themselves. The excursion into the world of make-believe began long before you saw the picture on the screen. It began as soon as you took your ticket stub and walked through the shiny brass doors. Particularly in the Stanley and Loew's there was a hush as you entered the majestic lobby, stepped onto the plush carpeting, and drank in the shimmer of lights and mirrors, the gold-leaf flourishes, the brocaded walls, the soft silken drapery, the old-world beauty of the statues and candelabra.

Even at the candy counter people ordered their non-parels and green leaves and Bon-Bons in just above a whisper. And the route to the balcony was a long winding staircase with a shiny brass railing, offering another perspective of the lobby. Once settled into a seat in the theater-a vast dark open space so different from today's narrow boxes-you could look up and see not a ceiling but a star-flecked sky, flickering blue dots in a field of soft black velvet.

These theaters were not just movie houses but showplaces in their own right. Kids entered them respectfully, and as we grew up they were legitimate places to take an "important date." On Saturday or Sunday nights it was not unusual to see couples dressed to the nines going to the movies at Journal Square. Because "going to the movies" at "'The Square" meant so much more than just seeing a film.

THE TWILIGHT LEAGUE

The Twilight Leagues gave men who would be kids a chance to play softball until no team would have them or until their legs just refused to chase another fly ball. These leagues also gave people a chance to relax after a hard day's work by watching a ball game in the open air.

Some nights these games would attract a couple hundred fans who stood along the foul lines and filled the small set of bleachers behind third base. Mike Balestieri, an invalid as long as I knew him, had a reserved spot. You'd always see him seated in his electric wheelchair in the shade of the shower house on the first base side. Each team had a small following of its own that would come to cheer, but at Oakley Oval the big favorite was the local team, the Alpines. (How a club in downtown Jersey City came to be known as the Alpines is something I could never figure out, but I never bothered to ask anyone.)

The Alpines had some fine players. Willie "Bruiser" was their pitcher, and he was really good. They had a guy named Ralphie "Giboff" who could hit the ball a ton. The only problem was he hit everything to left field and left field at this diamond went on for miles. So Ralphie was often just a long out, but what an out. "Gillie" Marsella was a steady shortstop, although he was moved to second when Vito

Monaco played. Vito was an ageless pepper pot who must have been fifty before he called it a career. One of the most colorful Alpines was Nicky "Perks," who played centerfield wearing a red bandana around his head.

The Alpines' perennial rival was St. Lucy's. They had some good ball players of their own, including a pot-bellied pitcher named "Junior" who was every bit as fast as Bruiser. St. Lucy's was led by a non-playing manager (rare for most teams), a guy by the name of Joe Dillon. Short and wiry with a whiskey complexion, Joe relished his position. He loved to came onto the field and argue with the umpires, a la Leo Durocher and Charlie Dressen. He'd rant and rave, his face reddening, but the umps would simply say, "Si-down, Joe." Undaunted, Joe would snap at them, "It's my per-rogative," to the delight of everyone in the crowd am on both teams. The by-play was often more fun than the games. One night St. Lucy's right fielder called in, "Hey, Joe, what's it two out?" "Two out," Joe screamed. "There ain't nobody out. What the hell game are you watchin'?"

I was a regular observer of the games played at Oakley Oval. One night when I was about 14, I was at the park early. Emerson Radio am TV was scheduled to play some rag-tag team that was in the cellar of the league. Now Emerson was an unusual team. They were the only team in the league that had full uniforms at a time when most teams had just hats, or maybe tee-shirts. Emerson was fully outfitted in black and orange, with those balloon pants that had little belts at the ankles. Most of the regular fans thought those uniforms silly and pretentious, so they usually rooted against Emerson. But because they played good ball, they got away with wearing the uniforms.

The team that Emerson was scheduled to play this particular night not only did not have uniforms, they didn't even have enough men. Without a win all season I guess it was hard for them to field a team each week. So they asked me if I could play and if I wanted to. I said "Sure."

Well, they put me in right field and batted me ninth. Emerson sent their number one pitcher home and took the field just to get in some practice. As fate would have it, this rag-tag team pulls out in front. I even walk and score a run. For the first time all season this team has a chance to win a game. And against the powerful and hated Emerson team! The fans who stayed are cheering for this great upset in the making.

Well, we go into the fifth inning with a two-run lead. Everybody is pumped up including our pitcher. But Emerson starts pecking away and they load the bases. It's two out and the batter hits a soft liner toward me in right-my first chance of the night. I come in a few steps and have a bead on it when I hear our second baseman running toward me. I take my eye off the ball to look at him but he says, "It's all yours, Kid." But when I look back at the ball the soft liner is sailing over my head. I chase it all the way to the chain link fence, turn and whip it back to the infield but much too late. Four runs score and so goes the dream of an underdog.

Boy, was I embarrassed. At the end of the inning I trotted back to a silent bench. Guys began taking off their spikes, even though we had last licks. One guy saw how dejected. I was and said, "Forget about it, Kid. We ain't won all year anyway." But I know he and his teammates would have liked to have won that one.

THE HOLY NAME PARADE

A major event in the church calendar was the Holy Name
Parade. Each fall the men and young men of all the churches in Jersey
City would march in open demonstration of their faith. Like Easter
Sunday and Christmas, the Holy Name Parade would bring out
parishioners whose faith was, shall we say, a much more private affair
with the lord than most priests would prefer. But they were there and
most welcome.

The men would gather in front of their respective churches, pick
up their little blue pennants bearing the Holy Name insignia, and form
ranks behind the parish priests who would be wearing cut-aways and
silk top hats. At the signal the barn would play and the march would
begin. First we'd parade through the streets of the parish, and people
would be out on their stoops or at the windows-women mostly-and
cheer as their sons and husbands and boyfriends marched by. If the
name of one of us was singled out by a girl no one else knew, that guy
would take quite a ribbing. I recall my Uncle Sonny and some of his
friends breaking into a formation of a cross when they passed the home
of one of their group. I never knew how they did it so quickly or so
well, but I guess it was their military training, since most had been in
the service. After marching through the parish, the unit would head for

Montgomery Street, to make the approach to Hudson Boulevard, where we'd join the rest of the city's men and head for the viewing stand in Lincoln Park.

There would often be delays, as we would have to wait for other downtown parishes to go by. During these delays many of the men would take advantage of the local tavern. (There was probably a tavern on every second block in the city, so finding one that was convenient was not difficult.) The men would often came back with sodas for us younger marchers and always with the score of the baseball game. The parade was usually held in the final weeks of the baseball season, sometimes on the final day, so baseball scores were important.

Marching up the steady incline of Montgomery Street on what often was a warm day could drain the enthusiasm out of the most zealous Christian marcher. But as we approached The Boulevard, one of the men would say: "OK, you guys, it's the Boulevard. Look smart." Jackets would be buttoned, pennants raised higher, and lines straightened out. Without anyone's saying it, we knew we'd be marching in front of people from various parishes and we wanted to make a good impression for ours. The Boulevard was packed on each side with women and girls from all over the city. It was quite a sight and quite a thrill when we'd be greeted by the cheers and applause of our own ladies.

The final leg of the march down the hill into the park and past the viewing stand seemed to go very quickly. There was silence in the ranks and a quickness in everyone's step. Then the lines would dissolve, same men would be met by their girlfriends, others would hop into cars brought to the park in the morning, and make their way through the traffic back home.

One of the interesting sidelights of the Holy Name Parade was that for this one day, parish rivalries created in the sports leagues and animosities formed along-lines of national heritage were suspended. For this one day we were all part of the same catholic community. We were all one.

THE NEIGHOORHOOD STORE

One of the great conveniences of city life is the neighborhood

store. Within a five-minute walk from our house were five grocery

stores, two bakeries, two dry cleaners, three candy stores, three barber

shops, and an army surplus store. It would take just ten minutes to get

to the butcher's, the bread store, the chicken market, the fish market, the

pastry shop, and any number of fruit and vegetable stands.

All were family businesses, run by storekeepers who'd cut you a

sliver of the provolone for you to sample. Frank the barber took no

money from kids but waited until their fathers came in for their

haircuts. Tony Monaco was a very friendly man who would "sing" the

items a customer requested. "Two quarts of milk for you," he'd sing as

he went to the case and brought back your milk.

In most of these stores, "bills" were calculated on the brown

paper bag you'd take your groceries home in. Tony, for example, would

use a black grease pencil to write down the price of each item. As he

wrote down the price he'd slide the item off to the side. He'd add up the

figures and total it on the bag. I don't recall anyone ever double

checking the addition before paying the bill. I'm sure they did it at

home though.

Also in most of these stores was a "trust" book, an early form of charge accounts. Most store-keepers were good about "trusting" their customers and would wait for their money until payday or until Pop found work. And there was no interest charged. It was all part of good will and neighborliness.

Further down was "Brunswick Street," a stretch of three or four blocks devoted to produce stores, the fish market, and the pastry shop. I was amazed one time to find the Jewish man behind the counter at Blum's quoting prices in Italian. Whatever it takes to do business!

The open air grocery stands were the scenes for many a battle of wills over the price of corn or tomatoes. Among the many things the supermarkets later destroyed was the great art of negotiation. "Too dear," was only the opening salvo in a shopper's quest to save some money, "That's cheap," would be the standard rejoinder from the shopkeeper, but certainly not the last word in the negotiation.

My brother-in-law Joe tells the story of his father's going to Brunswick Street late on a Saturday, just before closing. Pop got the owner down to fifteen cents for a cabbage. Then, figuring the man would have no use for the cabbage if he didn't sell it now, Pop pushed for another nickel off. Nine Saturdays nights out of ten that strategy would have worked. But the man had probably had a bad day or maybe a bad week. Or maybe he was just tired of haggling. For whatever reason, the storekeeper got so angry at that, he picked up the cabbage and smashed it in the street. "I'd rather throw it away than give it to you for a dime," the man said.

Besides the local stores, housewives also had other conveniences. For starters there was the milkman who brought two quarts of milk and a pint of cream to your door before you were out of bed in the morning. Women also bought much of their fruit and vegetables from peddlers who traveled the streets. In my earliest days I recall these peddlers coming around with horse-drawn wagons. Later the horses were replaced by trucks. Women would came down to the truck, prop their babies on a hip, and pick out their own produce without ever going more than ten yards from home. Some would even shop from their apartment windows. "How's the spinach today?" they'd shout down. "Good. Very fresh," the peddler would shout back. And He would fill the bag and send it up with a boy.

And do you remember the fish man? "A-tripp-o," he'd sing, announcing his presence and the fresh tripe he had for sale. "A-tripp-o, a-tripailo." Another man specialized in dairy products, bringing fresh ricotta and mozzarella right to the house.

Of course there was an A&P and many women, including my mother, did their real "heavy" shopping there, if they were up to a long walk or could convince dad to drive them with the car. But that was no more than once a week or every other week. In the meantime, what kept families going was the unique brand of personal service found at the neighborhood store.

SEASONS IN THE CITY

As kids growing up in the city, the seasons didn't mean the normal spring, summer, fall, winter. More often seasons referred to activities-baseball season, football season, and basketball season. And beyond these three standards, there were other, though shorter, seasons. For example, every year we had a yo-yo season. This generally was in September, when kids were back in school and looking for things to do at lunchtime. All of a sudden, completely unannounced, hundreds of these little round marvels would appear from nowhere, and all over the schoolyard kids would be "rocking the baby, " and. flinging the yo-yo "around the world. " You could do these tricks and make the yo-yo "sleep" if you could afford the 35 cents for the better article. But even if you had the plain one-trick variety, you worked that thing until your wrist got tired, or until the string broke, or your teacher confiscated it for playing with it in class. Or, simply because they got pretty boring after a few days, yo-yo season would end as mysteriously as it had begun.

Similar to yo-yo season was the "rick rack" season. Some people called it paddle ball. This consisted of a small rubber ball on the end of a long elastic stapled to a pan-shaped wooden paddle that fit snugly in your hand. The object was to hit the ball against the paddle as many times as you could without missing-great for hand-eye coordination. Most of these paddles were thin white plywood, selling for about ten cents. But I remember one season saving up for a red paddle of a little heavier wood that had a picture of a man riding a bucking bronco while whacking the ball against a paddle. I loved that thing and remember practicing for hours, counting each whack of the ball, trying to extend my prowess and the count each time. There was the conventional upward stroke, of course, but I was also getting pretty good at a side-angle stroke, and even could do a few behind the back. The problem with rick racks, though, was the elastic would break or slip out of the ball, and you'd have to secure the shortened elastic to the ball, usually with a sawed-off toothpick. This was just a temporary fix and in the midst of a good streak your ball might go flying across the schoolyard. Like the yo-yo, the rick rack could hold our attention for only so long, and then they would disappear. Where, I don't know because next year I could never find the old one.

Marble season was another short season. I recall two variations of marble games. One was to draw a circle in a patch of dirt and have each player put in a marble or two. Then from outside the circle each player would use his shooter to knock what he could out of the circle. The other variation was a single entry game at the curb. One of the reasons marbles was such a short season was that we played for keeps, and a really talented shooter could wipe out the rest of us quickly. And a pack of "mibs" was an expensive purchase back then. I had some help in this regard from my Uncle Nick. He worked for the DPW in those days pushing a broom, as did many others, to keep the city clean. Whenever he saw a lost marble he'd pick it up and save it for me. One of my first ambitions in life was to be a street cleaner, to get first crack at all those lost aggies.

Roller skating was a fair-weather season. Most kids would have a pair of metal skates that they'd attach to the bottom of their shoes. (Sneakers were no good because the clamps would slip off and you were forever borrowing a skate key to re-do them.) The skates were expandable so you could lend them around or use them for a few seasons as your foot got bigger. That is, if you didn't lose them first or use them for a scooter. Most roller skating was done in the street, and I recall the challenge and thrill of building up a head of steam and jumping over the manhole cover in the center of the street, or spreading my feet and skirting it daringly while whizzing by at a good clip. We could spend an entire Saturday flying around and doing the "whip" like Monta Jean Payne and Tuffy Brashun, roller derby stars we knew for a short time.

Bicycle season came in summer. Though bikes were used a lot for transportation, it was in summer that they became the focus of our play. "Going bike riding" meant three or four kids riding together down to the river or across town to see kids we hadn't seen since school closed. In summer you devoted time to your bike seriously. It was then that kids decided to paint their bikes, for instance. I remember taking great pains to tape a V on the ends of my fenders to paint a dashing white chevron on my newly painted black fenders. What class! In bicycle season we saved money for seat covers and reflectors and streamers and foxtails and fender flaps. Or we'd go the other way and "hot rod" the bike, turning the handle bars upward and removing the fenders and chain guard. I had more dungarees with teeth marks in the lower right leg after catching them in the chain.

Another summer season was scooters. These were usually home-made jobs fashioned from a length of two-by-four and a milk crate (made of wood and "borrowed" from a local deli.) For locomotion you'd split a roller skate, nailing one half to the front end of the two-by-four and the other to the rear. We'd nail two long, thin strips of wood to the top of the milk crate for handles.

Scooters were hard work to operate. You'd put one foot on the board and push yourself with the other until you'd built up enough speed to cruise. If your skate was fluid enough you could make same neat dips and tums with those things. Some kids painted their scooters and wrote names or numbers on them, or hammered bottle caps into the crate in all kinds of designs. Scooters were really a full-time activity, requiring a lot of patience, resourcefulness, energy, and imagination. As it think about it now, scooter season was fun.

SITTING ON THE STOOP

One of the pleasant past times of city-living was sitting on the stoop.

Recall a hot spell in July, perhaps the fifth or sixth consecutive day of

90 degree heat. The heat is now locked in the tiny apartments, encased

by the heat in the apartments above and below and in the buildings

standing shoulder to shoulder on the right and left. Even as the

thermometer slips slightly in the evening, the temperature in the

apartment stays oppressively the same.

But the apartment-dweller does find relief--on the front stoop. I

can recall walking to meet my friends on summer evenings and feeling

as if I were walking in review of people sitting on every stoop in the

neighborhood. Those were the days before the folding aluminum chair,

when people sat on the stone steps, sometimes moving the air in front

of them with a straw fan or newspaper. Occasionally you'd see a

wooden kitchen chair or a cushion or two, but generally people sat on

the stone, itself still warm with the day's heat. They'd sit and watch and

talk, and breathe a collective sigh if even the slightest of breezes blew

by.

It seemed people had different shifts for sitting on the stoop.

Shortly after supper the men would come out, fed and washed after a

mucky day on the job. They'd sit in sleeveless undershirts smoking a pipe or reading a newspaper. Some might get the hose out and wash down the sidewalk and hope they themselves would cool off in the process. In minutes, though, puffs of steam would begin to rise from the concrete drying quickly in the heat. Some of the men would keep an eye on their younger children who rode their tricycles up and down the block, oblivious to the heat though rings of dirt formed around their necks in perspiration. The kids sensed the lateness of the hour and knew that for same reason they were allowed to stay out later than usual, but they were not about to ask why. They'd enjoy it as long as they could. And if Pop bought them a Good Humor, well, the perfect topping to a perfect day.

Sometime after the men, the women would come down, after the supper dishes had been washed and put away, and the kitchen straightened up. Their hair brushed back and their housedresses still damp, they'd usually sit at the top step, for this would be only a moment's respite. They, too, needed to rest their hot, tired bodies, while perhaps watching the falling sun cast a fiery glow over Dickinson High School. Soon, however, they would realize the hour and shepherd their young ones upstairs to bath and bed.

Their husbands would follow in a short while, and in the later hours the stoops would belong to the young men, the bachelors who still lived at home and their married peers. They might share a beer or ice cream; sometimes they'd listen to a baseball game or prize fight on a portable radio. I can recall sitting on the stoop with some of my older cousins. I'd came home at the required time and let my parents know I was there and would be on the stoop for a while.

My cousins Andy and J.D. would let me stay and I'd sit quietly and listen to them talk about their jobs, about politics, about their army experiences. As darkness settled, it seemed the conversations would get softer and more serious. I once heard them discussing a young man from the neighborhood who had taken his own life right up the street in the ballpark where I'd often play. Despite the weather, I felt chills that night.

As a young teenager I spent practically an entire summer of evenings on Pat Marcella's stoop. Pat lived just around the block from where I did and I seldom saw her during the day. (What did teenage girls do during the day that kept them out of sight?) But at night Pat and JoAnn and Mario and I would congregate on Pat's stoop and talk. It was a time to shift from the mind-set of the day-sports am games-to that of other things--boy-girl things. Of course, Mario and I played macho sometimes, but after spending so much time with these two girls, the facades came down one by one and we were just ourselves.

People who lived in Pat's house, mostly relatives, didn't seem to mind having to snake through us as they left or entered the building, and we never saw our being there as a nuisance to anyone. Because all we were doing was sitting on the stoop and talking, an accepted custom on summer evenings in the city.

HOLY ROSARY SCHOOL

I guess I always liked school, grammar school, that is. I was good at it, I had friends there, and so I went eagerly. My feeling of security in school stemmed in part from the fact that my older brother Jack had paved the way for me. He was a good student, respected by kids and teachers, so when I came along I guess people expected more of the same. For the most part, that's what they got.

My memories of grammar school are not of lessons learned but of occasions to be with kids and do things. The stamp of the nuns on many of those things was clear. One of them was the plays. It seems we were always rehearsing for some kind of show-for a feast day, a holiday, or the big commencement program in the spring. We began rehearsals for that around October 15th. For most of these extravaganzas, each class did a scene from "'The Mikado," some songs, or a skit or something.

For so much of my "theatrical career," however, I was pulled from the regular class production and inserted into an Italian special. I knew not a word of Italian and the nuns never thought to explain to me what I was saying or singing. They just gave me the script, taught me the words, and drilled me over and over until I memorized them. I guess I was good at picking up the pronunciation, particularly the rolling r's. Mom recalls with all the objectivity of a stage mother how brilliant I was at the age of seven pleading my love in Italian to my "Cara Rosina," played by five year old Annie Vesper. What I remember about that routine were my props-a cane and a black derby stuffed with paper to keep it above my eyes.

I remember, too, running around the school yard at lunchtime. On a single day I had to go home to change three times. Once I fell on the ice and tore my pants; no sooner did I get back to school but I slipped on the oil that was being pumped into the tank beneath the ground. Mom had run out of good pants to give me, and I had to return to school wearing my brother Jack's pants, which needless to say were swimming on me, since Mom always bought our clothes "a little big" so we had roam to grow into them.

One day when I was in about sixth or seventh grade, Father Livolsi came into class and told Sister he needed five boys for a special project that would probably take us out of class for the rest of the day. I was thrilled to be picked as one of the five and even more excited when I found out what the project was--a game at Yankee Stadium.

Catholic nuns have become infamous for their tendencies toward capital punishment, and I guess the nuns at our school were typical of most. With 40 or 50 kids in a class, however, and sometimes more, I guess they had to rely on force or the threat of it to survive. Though the spanking machine in the Principal's office was never verified, a ruler across the knuckles was a frequent attention getter. Kneeling was a popular punishment, sometimes with arms outstretched, if the crime warranted. My handwriting was always poor and once in the very low grades I had a particularly sloppy paper pinned to my tie. I then had to make the rounds of all the classes to show my "chicken scratch," as sister called it, to the entire school. Fortunately a more kindly nun intervened after three or four stops. Maybe that day somehow had something to do with me becoming a writer. Maybe it's called defiance. Though these methods have been pretty much discarded now-and rightfully so-I don't recall anyone being emotionally or physically scarred by them. There was a fear of sorts in the air, yes, but a Reign of Terror it was not.

One nun, however, was feared by everyone, including the other nuns. This was Sister Violet. A frail, diminutive woman who spoke hardly above a whisper and barely rustled the air when she moved, Sister Violet was the school superintendent or regional supervisor or something. Once a year she'd come to examine the school. For days before her arrival the sisters would warn us that "Sister Violet was coming." Had it been Josef Stalin himself I don't think there would have been such a stir. Bulletin boards would get fresh displays; we'd do easy assignments on the "best" paper that Sister could post around the room. And I vaguely remember going over the same lesson for two or three days, which we just happened to be doing again when Sister Violet came to observe our class.

One thing that I don't think has changed at parish schools is the need for fund-raising. We were always hawking chance books, raffles, carnivals, bazaars, card parties. But tuition then was about fifty cents a month, so we really couldn't complain. And we always were encouraged to practice Christian charity. Donating money to rescue a mission baby from the wilds of paganism was a constant throughout my years at Holy Rosary.

Another fund-raiser was afternoon movies. Classes would be canceled and for a quarter we'd see a full-length movie right in the school auditorium. To increase the revenue, I guess, we were allowed to take younger brothers and sisters of pre-school age to these movies, and I remember once bringing my brother Joe. But the girls made too much of a fuss over him so I never did that again. More than once we saw "Keys of the Kingdom" with Gregory Peck, but the movies weren't always religious. I remember seeing the original "Zorro" in school, with Tyrone Power as Don Diego. On the way home that day all the kids were writing Z's in the air with imaginary swords. If a movie included a kissing scene, the sisters always knew how to do something to the projector to blur those frames.

Valentine's Day was special in school, with kids exchanging cards am then tallying them up to see who got the most. We'd dress up for Halloween, and have a party for Christmas, and baskets for Easter. On Mother's and Father's days the sisters would write a special message on the board which we'd copy, again on the "best" paper. We'd painstakingly glue these to construction paper, making an artistic acknowledgement of gratitude to our parents. The End-products never seemed indicative of the time and effort that went into these cards, but the idea of doing something special for Mam and Dad did reach us. Thinking back on it now, I guess I do recall some of the lessons the good sisters taught.

THE MULTI-PURPOSE RUBBER BALL

Growing up in the city, you didn't need a lot of money to keep busy. A quarter for a rubber ball would be all you'd need for hours and hours of fun.

The rubber ball I remember was about two and a half inches in diameter and was made of hard but resilient pink rubber. Stamped on it was the name of its manufacturer, Spalding Rubber Co. Hence the name "Spaldeen." For a short time the fashion was a slightly smaller and softer ball, a fusion of two different colored pieces of rubber, usually blue and yellow. But we stopped using these trendy balls because they split too easily. One good crack with a stickball bat would sheer them in two.

With the Spaldeen, however, you could play stickball for days, if you didn't lose it first. And lose it you might because a reasonably new Spaldeen could really sail. Besides stickball, the Spaldeen was ideal for other games. If you were alone, you could play stoopball. You'd throw the ball against a stoop, and if you caught the carom on the fly it was an out. An error or grounder by you put a man on first. If the ball hit the point and soared over your head, home run.

With a friend you could use the Spaldeen for box tennis, a city version of table tennis without table or paddles. The squares in a sidewalk would serve as the net and boundaries, and you'd hit the ball with your hands. This game required dexterity and quick reactions. Same kids could put same wicked English on that old Spaldeen. Another game for two involved placing a Popsicle stick midway between yourself and your opponent. You toss the ball at the stick, counting the number of times you hit it. A game with more excitement and more people was Ball Tag. Instead of tagging someone with your hand, you'd throw the ball at him. If you hit him he was "it." He might also have the Spaldeen imprint on his back for a few days.

Then, too, there was wall-ball. You found a tall wall that was fairly smooth and unobstructed by windows, such as a garage or school, and threw the ball against the wall, as high and as hard as you could. The object was to get the ball over your opponent's head or hope he'd miss it for an error and a run.

With a big group of kids we'd play punchball. For this you'd need a schoolyard, so you could actually set up a diamond, with bases. The batter would stand at the plate, toss the ball above his head and punch it with his fist. The defense, with as many infielders and outfielders as could be mustered, would play the ball as in a baseball game. How I envied those kids who could consistently punch that pink rubber ball high and deep, challenging even the best outfielders.

A real fast and exciting game was boxball, a variation of baseball played at a street intersection. The storm drains at the corners were the bases and the defense would have a pitcher and infielders only. That was the real challenge, as any ball through the infield was usually a home run. The pitcher stood literally in the middle of the intersection and tossed the ball on a single bounce to the plate. The batter could punch or slap the ball and try to beat out a hit. With the short distance between the bases, balls could come screaming at an infielder's feet. He'd have to make a clean pick-up am a quick, accurate throw to first to get the sprinting runner. The runner would have to be agile, too, touching first and then skipping the curb without bashing his shins against the hard steel of the storm drain frame.

And, of course, if you and a friend just wanted to while away the time without being competitive, you could just have a catch. You'd just toss the ball back and forth easily as you talked about things kids talked about, or you'd stand in the street and throw long high flies to one another until you got tired or until it got too dark to see that little pink rubber ball.

THE CANDY STORE

One of the cornerstones of life in Jersey City was the neighborhood candy store. For some it was the gathering place. For little kids, the candy store was where we learned to make tough decisions.

Leaning against the glass showcase and caressing the nickel in your sweaty little palm, you learn about trade-offs, such as the scrumptious delight of chocolate and raisins in the tiny trapezoid of the Chunky versus the longer-lasting but rather boring Sugar Daddy or Bonomo's Turkish Taffy. With only a nickel to spend you considered the alternatives. A box of Good and Plenty (Bad and Not Enough) could last an afternoon, but Ju Ju Bees could last all day. They'd also stick between your teeth for a week. Of course there were those strips of paper with coated little drops on them, about a hundred to a sheet. Very economical-a penny or two for a sheet, but I could never get the drops completely free of the paper.

Green leaves were good but Chuckles were better. But there were only six Chuckles in a package, (counting the black one,) not a prudent choice on a five-cent budget. Crackerjacks were a sure buy for a while. The large box suggesting an all-day treat and the sweet crunchy taste of the sticky popcorn would lure any kid. And the mystery in the prize buried away was often too much for us to resist. In time, however, we outgrew the prizes, or at least pretended we did, and moved on to more adult candy like Hershey Bars and Almond Joys. Raisinettes were my favorite candy, and still are. The solution might be a penny's worth of a number of goodies, such as malt balls, gummy hats, licorice sticks, and then maybe a pretzel or two.

You learned about storekeepers at a young age in the city. Some would know what we were going through in deciding what to buy with that nickel, which might be the last for some time. These men or women would let you browse the store, discuss the purchase with your friend, perhaps decide on two items you both liked which you'd then share. Other storekeepers had never been kids and didn't like kids in the store. (Then why'd they go into the candy store business in the first place? Who'd they expect to attract with the likes of chocolate-covered marshmallow bars and wax teeth?) These people would say, "Are ya buyin' or just look.in'? I ain't got all day." Kids, as I said, learned quickly the stores they would patronize.

The candy store was the oasis on a hot summer afternoon. After a game of stickball, we'd escape from the heat in the cool darkness of Joe Paone's Candy Store, later known as Corky's. We'd open the heavy lid of the soda case and lower our heads to feel the cool caress of the icy water. Joe would fill the case with soda and lay cakes of ice right on the bottles. As the day got hotter the ice would melt but the water would stay icy cold for a long time. We'd lower a hand into the water, up to the elbow practically, and allow the chilling sensation to run throughout the arm, soon cooling the rest of the body. We'd do this three or four times in trying to decide on the soda. Will it be the ever-popular Coca Cola? Or the larger though gassier Pepsi? Or how about a Royal Crown Cola? I could never seem to finish a Royal Crown without feeling like a float in the Macy's Parade. 7-up didn't quite do it for kids, and neither did Yoo Hoo chocolate, until later on. There was also the Nehi collection-orange and later grape. It wasn't easy making a choice.

Sometimes we'd look at other items in the candy store. Willie's, for example, had the best collection of comic books. Located in the back of his store, the comic books were in no organized arrangement but just seemed to be strewn around like items on the "bargain" table in a department store. So you had to wade through them and in the process could catch up on Archie and the sexy girls of Riverdale High or on the latest Superman adventure. You might spend an hour there and have gotten your fill of comics, and walk out without buying anything.

If you happened to have some big money you might look at toys, such as the Rick Racks, which the rest of the world called Paddle Ball. Or those little boxes with BB's inside, which you try to maneuver gingerly into a pattern of holes. And if you weren't that hungry for candy or thirsty for soda, or flush enough for a toy or game, or interested in reading, there were always gum and baseball cards.

Yes, the neighborhood candy store--an institution in city life.

THE CHURCH

The church was an important element in the lives of many people in Jersey City. You knew a boy and girl were serious about each other when they started going to ten o'clock mass together. It wasn't unusual to see long lines of people waiting outside the confessional on Saturday afternoons, kids in their play clothes. .And someone once said that if the church didn't run its dances and parties, most of the people in Jersey City would have turned to stone.

I became an altar boy when I was in fourth grade, at a time when the church was shrouded in an air of mystery. I had wanted to become an altar boy since I first saw Tony Fraacchio, an eighth-grader, waltz around the altar with such grace am style, his heels clicking smartly on the tile of the sanctuary. In those days the priest and his helpers were turned away from the congregation and I recall Tony's kneeling at the foot of the priest unhesitatingly responding the Latin prayers. He was engaged in an inscrutable dialogue with the priest, and I wanted to be a part of it.

At the time I became an altar boy I was barely tall enough to reach the top of the altar. One of the altar boy's major tasks in the "old" mass was to move the priest's missal from the Epistle Side to the Gospel side and then back again. I'd strain to slide the mammoth red missal off the altar, then do a Charlie Chaplin under its weight as I carried it down the steps and up again. Just trying to keep my balance was problem enough but I also had to keep from tripping on the hem of my cassock, which was usually too long for me, since I was shorter than most of the other kids when I first started serving. But I loved serving mass. I'd jump at the chance of serving extra masses on Saturdays when the older kids would say they "couldn't make it."

I remember the cold winter mornings getting up for the seven o'clock mass. My father would wake me about six-thirty, and I'd wash in our unheated bathroom and dress quickly. If it was very cold out and I had time, he would wait for me and drive me to church. I remember leaning against the steel of our coal-burning stove, with my coat on, letting its warmth run through my body. On other days, I'd pull the collar of my coat up around my neck, bow my head to the wind, and walk in the dark of the morning the three and a half blocks to church.

When I got there, John, the sexton, was always in the sacristy, either asleep in a chair or pacing impatiently if Father Santora happened to be late. Which was rare. Most mornings Fr. Santora was there not only early but also bright and chipper, his shoes bearing their ever-present shine. Corny jokes were his forte when he was in the right mood.

I recall one incident, though, when Fr. Santora showed his other side. It was at an evening service, probably a special novena. I was not on the altar but in the first pew with my friend Brother Ricciuto and only a few other altar boys. Father Santora took his preaching seriously am he was good at it. This one night he was waxing hot and in the course of his talk said something about the Turks. For same reason Brother and I thought that was funny. We burst out laughing and Fr. Santora glanced down at us coldly. We checked our laughter but despite our efforts, only temporarily. It was one of those moments when self-control was worth twenty dollars an ounce and the thing we wanted to do most was control our laughter, but we just couldn't. Father glared at me and pointed toward the door. My uncontrollable laughter died instantly.

I slowly got up and said, "Let's go, Brother." But my pal swerved his legs aside to give me roam to pass. I exited the pew at the center aisle and had to pass in front of Father, who had stopped talking and was waiting for me to leave. I sensed the eyes of everyone in church on me and felt the blood rushing to my head like lava. It was a long, long walk to the side door of the church. After that night I gave Fr. Santora a wide berth for quite a while.

The days I liked most were just before Easter. When I was an altar boy Holy Week services were held in the early morning as early as five o'clock. Maybe because of the early hour, the sense of mystery in the church was especially keen. It began with my waking early and walking to church in the dead of night, the streets still and peaceful, the neighborhood sound asleep. Other boys might already be there or would soon follow and I'd feel a real sense of belonging, membership in a club that met while the rest of the world slept. We'd line up accenting to height for the procession and Father Vitale, who was in charge of the altar boys, would say: "Angelo, get up here. You're too short to be way back there." Minutes later he'd say, "Angelo, get back here." We all concluded Angelo Flora had a rubber neck. The church was empty those mornings except for a handful of old ladies who seemed never to go home. Few lights were on but the flicker from the candles dotted the darkness and the aroma of burning candle wax filled the church. The services were not only long but very different from the standard. There was much chanting, in Latin of course, and readings from old books bound in hard somber covers.

After services on Holy Thursday we'd quickly get out of our cassocks and begin bringing potted lilies from the basement to literally cover the sanctuary with them. The nuns would be there directing the operation and decorating the altar in white silk. In the middle of the sanctuary we would place tall candles in red and blue glass cylinders in the shape of a cross. For the rest of the day altar boys in pairs would be stationed near the cross to take requests from people to light the candles. It was a tradition at the time for Catholics to visit an odd number of churches on Holy Thursday, and our church was one of the most beautiful and most visited in the area. So in addition to taking my turn to light the candles I also spent a good part of the day roaming downtown visiting churches I did not enter on any other day of the year.

When I returned early the next morning for Good Friday services, the altar would have been stripped bare of all flowers, candles, and practically everything else. The change, I think, had a powerful impact on me in conveying the solemnity and meaning of Good Friday. The bareness of the altar, in contrast to the spectacle of the previous day, was effective in subduing even the most boisterous of our group.

Holy Saturday was a festive day. After the early morning service, which was a little later and a little lighter, we knew Lent was over. People would came to the side of the church to fill jars with the freshly blessed holy water for the that were placed on bedroom walls in the home. Lent was over and with it the fasting and the abstinence from candy or movies and such.

Easter Sunday, to be honest, was more a social event than a religious one. That was the day most kids wore new clothes. The girls would wear new dresses and spring coats, with cute little straw bonnets. The boys would wear new suits and shoes. I remember the year iridescent colors were the rage and kids came to church with flaming pink ties am matching socks. Same of the younger kids wore little felt fedoras, cut-down imitations of dad's hat. So many people came to church on Easter Sunday that extra masses were said in the school hall. The children's mass was said there and I remember enjoying the fashion show watching all the girls decked out in their Easter finery parading up to the stage to receive communion.

But even on ordinary Sundays, it was nice going to a church you knew, to hear priests you knew, to see people you knew. People felt comfortable there, most sitting in the same section of the church-the same pew, even-week after week. The church and mass on Sunday were in our roots, another constant in our lives that made us feel the world made sense and that we were part of something larger than ourselves, part of something that would last.

TALKIN' BASEBALL

Living so close to New York, people in Jersey City were

drenched in baseball. When we weren't playing the game, we were

probably talking about the Giants, Dodgers, or Yankees. With three

"local" teams, the rivalries were fierce and the arguments endless. Fans

of all ages would approach hysteria arguing the superiority of their

teams-records not withstanding- and of their favorite centerfielder-

Willie Mays, Duke Snider, or Mickey Mantle. We'd use statistics on

home runs and strikeouts (same of us knew more about baseball players

than we'd ever know about anything else), exploits now exaggerated

tenfold, and other kinds of "evidence." Often, however, the argument

would resort to personal attacks against the other player, brilliant wit

such as "he stinks."

I was a Giant fan since I first knew anything about baseball

because my brother Jack was a Giant fan, and so were my cousins, Jack

and Andrew, who lived in the same house we did. Their father,

however, was a Yankee fan, and the arguments that poor man had to

endure were legendary. I guess Uncle Frank could afford to be patient

with us upstarts because throughout the 1950's the Yanks were always

winning. "Lucky," we'd say, "the Yankee luck again." If the Yankees

did lose a game I'd look forward to rubbing it in. But Uncle Frank wouldn't get upset. He'd just say, "Tightening up the league, Kippy.

They're just tightening up the league." When I persisted, as I often did,

and he tired of it, he'd sometimes say, "What the hell do you know?

You still have the ring of the pot on your ass." I had no rejoinder for

that.

One of the most talked about baseball games of all times was

"the Bobby 'Thomson game." This was the third and final playoff game

in 1951 that won the pennant for the Giants. The Dodgers had led the

league all season but in mid-August the Giants made their move and

finally tied Brooklyn on the last day of the season. After splitting the

first two playoff games, they squared off for the pennant in the third

game at the Polo Grounds.

It was a school day and after school I raced home to watch the

game on television. But instead I had to run an errand for my mother.

In those days Mom worked at home beading sweaters and my brother

Jack and I shared the dreaded task of taking Mom's completed work to

what we called "the beading store" and picking up a new batch of

patterns and beads. This meant riding the No. 9 bus all the way up to

West Side Avenue, enduring the "oohs and aahs" of the women who

did the same work as Mom but on site, and then taking the bus home

again. As luck would have it, it was my tum on this day of the third and final playoff game. After pleading about the importance of the game and my obligation to the Giants to be there, I took up the bag and made my way to the bus.

Fortune did smile on me, however, when I was waiting for the bus for the return trip. The bus stop opposite the beading store was outside a tavern, and naturally the patrons were watching the ballgame on TV. The door was open so I timidly poked my head in to get the score. Nobody shooed me away, since they were all interested in the game, so I took a few steps and actually entered the bar itself. There in that dark and dank saloon with the overpowering smell of beer enveloping me, I saw the ending to perhaps baseball's most exciting game.

No need to repeat the details here of how the Dodgers took a lead into the ninth, of how Whitey I.ockman broke his ankle sliding into third, of how Ralph Branca was brought in from the bullpen to slam the door on the Giant rally, of how Bobby Thomson hit the shot heard 'round the world. Images are etched forever in the of baseball fans-images of Jackie Robinson looking up for the fly ball that was snatched away by the overhang in leftfield, of Leo Durocher hugging Thomson at third base, of the two of them hopping together to the plate, of the entire Giant team descending on the Flying Scot. And in our ears

will forever ring the sweet words of Russ Hodges:

"The Giants win the pennant! The Giants win the pennant! The Giants

win the pennant!"

We're still talkin' about it.

SUMMERTIME

Summertime for a kid growing up in the city was life at its best. It was truly a life of leisure, a life lived for the moment. Wake up when you feel like it; dawdle or run right out, depending on your mood; play or just hang around the neighborhood with your friends. The great thing about the city was, even when you had nothing to do, you always had someone to do it with.

I remember summer mornings being hot, waking to find the sun pouring into my room. It didn't bother me, though. After a leisurely breakfast I'd dress in dungarees (not jeans then), polo shirt, and sneakers, and go out to see what the day would bring. A short stroll around the comer and I'd more than likely find my friend Mario or Sox or Richie Mack. They might be playing cards (Casino, mostly-pronounced casina) or Camelot, a game Richie would bring out because he was good at it. A tall, skinny kid with shiny blond hair, he wasn't much at sports, so he liked to play Camelot. We'd sit on the steps of the Alpine club, or on somebody's bench nearby, and play. Quite a few people had benches in front of their houses and didn't mind you're using them if you didn't make too much noise. We might flip baseball cards for a while or just jabber like old ladies.

After a while, someone would suggest stickball and we'd go up the street. With chalk we'd draw a box on the shower house to serve as home plate, as pitchers threw hard, baseball-style. Stickball was great because all you needed was one other kid and you could have a game. A rubber ball and a broom handle was all the equipment necessary. Of course, you needed a good eye am quick hands to land that thin broom handle on the ball traveling at a good clip.

When the city got unbearably hot, one of the few ways to cool off was the fire hydrant, or Johnny Pump, as we called it. You might be sitting around languidly when all of a sudden you'd hear "WHOOSH," the sound of water gushing from the fire hydrant at the corner. Someone-usually an older kid with guts and access to a wrench, sometimes an adult, but no one ever revealed who actually did it-would loosen the cap on the front of the hydrant, turn the valve on top, and release the cool, refreshing water. Kids would came quickly from all over the neighborhood to stand under the cool spray made by a bigger kid squatting in front of the hydrant, his behind creating a spray that could reach quite a distance if he was skilled enough and had a big enough behind.

Some kids went home for bathing suits, but usually there was no time for that. Kick off your shoes and jump in because you knew that in a matter of minutes the police car would pull up and shut the hydrant. If it was real hot, the cops seemed to take their time, to give us kids-am the adults who stood around enjoying the errant spray-a slight respite from the heat. As quickly as the water frolic began, it was over. Same of the little kids would "swim" around in the water that backed up over the catch basin on the corner, but everyone else went back to what they were doing. But we were at least a little cooler for a while.

Same afternoons, I'd return home to watch baseball on TV with my brother. Most major league baseball was played in the sunlight in those days. I especially liked watch "Happy Feltons' Knothole Gang" before Dodger games. How I envied those kids who got to field grounders hit by major leaguers at Ebbets Field. I watched the Giants religiously, including Laraine Day's pre-game show, "A Day with the Giants," and the post-game show, hosted by the Fordham Flash, Frankie Frisch. When the Giants would lose, the Flash would moan: "Oh, those bases on balls." He seemed to have Whitey Lockman on the show a lot, and each tin-e he'd ask the same question: "Whitey, what's your toughest play?" (It was the 3-6-3 double play.)

One time Frankie was interviewing Roy Campanella of the hated Dodgers. The Flash said he noticed Roy to the Giants hitters, obviously trying to distract them. "What do you say, Roy, to Willie Mays when he's at the plate?" Roy smiled. "I say a lot of things but I usually get to him when I say, 'Willie, you married?"

After supper, I'd usually watch the softball up at "The Oaks," then go around to the comer. We might play boxball in the street, using the four catch basins (which we called sewers) as bases. Sometimes the ball would roll down into the basin and without hesitation we'd lift the grid, and one of us would lie down, face in the basin, to retrieve the ball. Depending on where it was, the others might have to hold the retriever by his feet and dip hint way down into the basin. Such faith in one's fellow man! Only if it were full with water did we have a real distaste for this.

Some nights we'd play kick the can or ring-o-levio and other types of street games. If we were in the mood for excitement, we might stand in the doorway of Willie's candy store on Monmouth Street and shout, "Willie the Jew with the bald head," and then run like the wind. We'd hear Willie's response, "You're God was a Jew" trailing after us. We might walk down to DiFeo's for a lemon ice or up to Dairy Queen. Often we'd just sit around and talk until it was time to go in. The events of the day would be completely forgotten and not a single thought was given to tomorrow. Summertime--that was indeed a peaceful life.

In fact, thinking back on all of these memories, and on the many that just dally in my mind and never make it onto paper, I realize that the first dozen or so years of my life were like one long summer vacation. Sure, the years between then and now filter out the harshness and struggles, but what's left to remember is an abundance of warm, happy days with close, caring people, sharing the same unpretentious lifestyle in a way that made it fun to be a kid growing up in Jersey City. I had fun then, and I had fun reliving those days here in this little book. I hope you did too.